winners & losers

by Sydney J. Harris

D0950217

ARGUS COMMUNICATIONS   Niles, Illinois 60648

Text © 1968 Sydney J. Harris and
    © 1964, 1965, 1966, 1967 Publishers Newspaper Syndicate
Illustrations © 1973 Argus Press, Inc.

Jacket Design and Book Illustrations by Nicole Hollander

Argus Communications
7440 Natchez Avenue
Niles, Illinois 60648

International Standard Book Number: 0-913592-21-8
Library of Congress Catalog Card Number: 73-78534

TABLE OF CONTENTS

scoreboard one

A winner
makes commitments;
a loser
makes promises.

When **a winner**
makes a mistake,
he says,
"I was wrong";
when **a loser**
makes a mistake,
he says,
"It wasn't my fault."

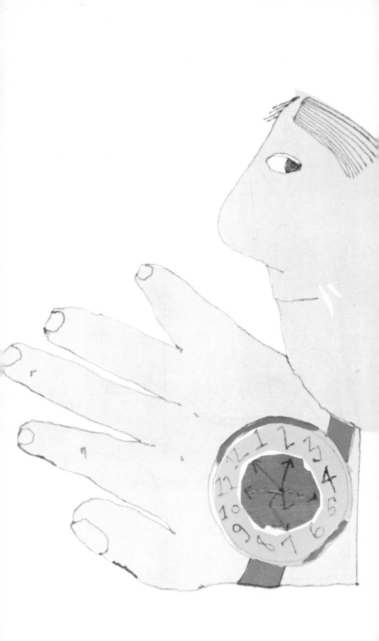

A winner
works harder than a loser,
and has more time;
a loser
is always "too busy"
to do what is necessary.

A winner
isn't nearly as afraid
of losing
as **a loser**
is secretly
afraid of winning.

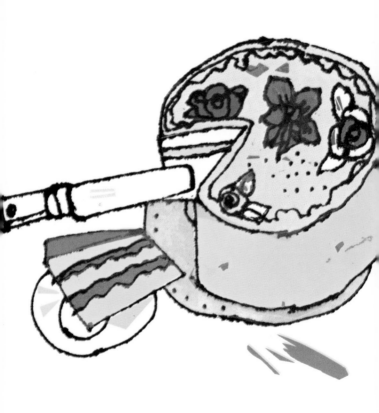

A winner
goes *through* a problem;
a loser
goes *around* it,
and never gets past it.

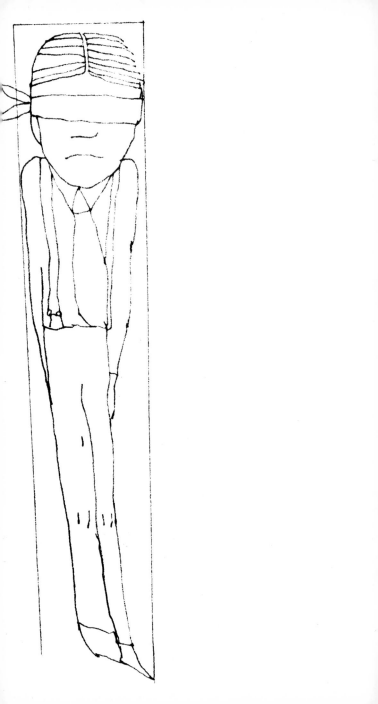

A winner says,
"Let's find out";
a loser says,
"Nobody knows."

A *winner*
knows what to fight for,
and what to compromise on;
a loser
compromises
on what he shouldn't,
and fights for
what isn't worthwhile
fighting about.

A winner
shows he's sorry
by making up for it;
a loser
says, "I'm sorry,"
but does the same thing
the next time.

A winner
would rather be admired
than liked,
although he would prefer both;
a loser
would rather be liked
than admired,
and is even willing to pay
the price of mild contempt
for it.

A *winner* listens;
a loser just waits
until it's his turn
to talk.

A winner
feels strong enough
to be gentle;
a loser
is never gentle—
he is either weak
or pettily tyrannous
by turns.

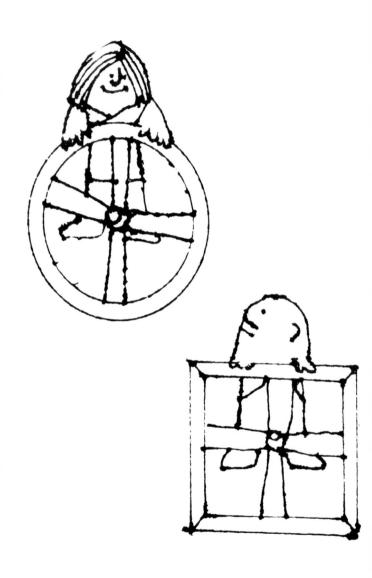

A winner says,
"There ought to be
a better way to do it";
a loser says,
"That's the way
it's always been done here."

A winner
respects those
who are superior to him,
and tries to learn
something from them;
a loser
resents those
who are superior to him,
and tries to find
chinks in their armor.

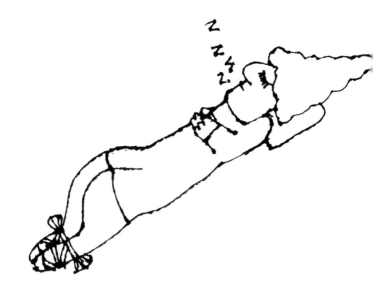

A winner
paces himself;
a loser
has only two speeds:
hysterical and lethargic.

scoreboard two

A winner
knows when the price
of winning
comes too high;
a loser
is overly eager
to win
what he cannot handle
or keep.

A winner
has a healthy appreciation
of his abilities,
and a keen awareness
of his limitations;
a loser
is oblivious
both of his true abilities
and his true limitations.

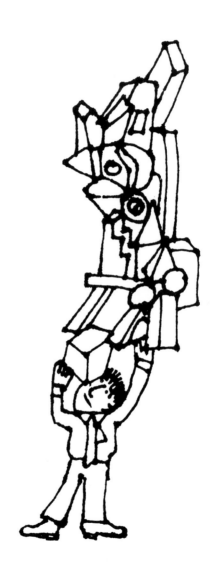

A winner
takes a big problem
and separates it into smaller parts
so that it can
be more easily manipulated;
a loser
takes a lot of little problems
and rolls them together
until they are unsolvable.

A winner
knows that people
will be kind
if you give them the chance;
a loser
feels that people
will be unkind
if you give them the chance.

A *winner* focuses;
a *loser* sprays.

A winner
learns from his mistakes;
a loser
learns only
not to make mistakes
by not trying anything
different.

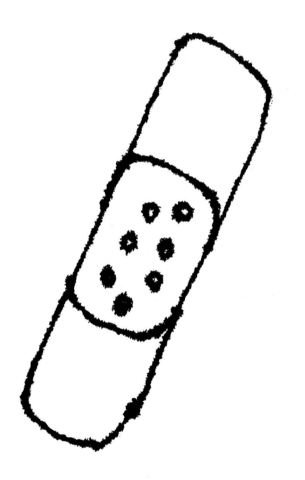

A winner
tries never to hurt people,
and does so only rarely,
when it serves a higher purpose;
a loser
never wants to hurt people
intentionally,
but does so all the time,
without even knowing it.

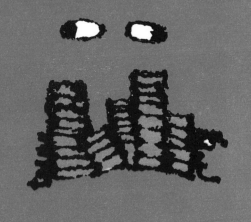

A winner
uses amassing only
as a means to enjoying;
a loser
makes amassing an end in itself—
therefore, no matter
how much the loser amasses,
he never looks upon himself
as a winner,
and he never is.

A *winner*
is sensitive
to the atmosphere around him ;
a loser
is sensitive
only to his own feelings.

scoreboard three

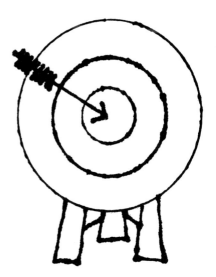

A loser
blames "politics"
or "favoritism"
for his failure;
a winner
would rather blame himself
than others—
but he doesn't waste much time
on any kind of blame.

A loser
believes in "fate";
a winner
believes that we make our fate
by what we do,
or fail to do.

A loser
feels cheated
if he gives more than he gets;
a winner
feels that he is simply building up
credit for the future.

A loser
becomes bitter
when he's behind,
and careless
when he's ahead;
a winner
keeps his equilibrium
no matter which position
he happens to find himself in.

A loser
is afraid
to acknowledge his defects
to himself
or to others;
a winner
is aware
that his defects are part
of the same central system
as his assets,
and while he tries to diminish
their effect,
he never denies
their influence.

A loser
smolders
with unexpressed resentment
at bad treatment,
and revenges himself
by doing worse;
a winner
freely expresses resentment
at bad treatment,
discharges his feelings,
and then forgets it.

A loser
prides himself
on his "independence"
when he is merely being contrary,
and prides himself
on his "teamwork"
when he is merely being conformist
a winner
knows which decisions
are worth an independent stand,
and which
should be gone along with.

A loser
is envious of winners
and contemptuous of other losers;
a winner
judges others only by how well
they live up to their own capacities,
not by some external scale
of worldly success,
and can have more respect
for a capable shoeshine boy
than for a crass opportunist.

A loser
thinks there are rules
for winning and losing;
a winner
knows that every rule in the book
can be broken,
except one —
be who you are,
and become all you were meant to be,
which is the only winning game
in the world.

A loser
leans on those
stronger than himself,
and takes out his frustrations'
on those weaker than himself;
a winner
leans on himself,
and does not feel imposed upon
when he is leaned on.

scoreboard four

A winner
seeks for the goodness
in a bad man,
and works with that part of him;
a loser
looks only for the badness
in a good man,
and therefore finds it hard
to work with anyone.

A winner
admits his prejudices,
and tries to correct for them
in making judgments;
a loser
denies his prejudices,
and thus becomes
their lifelong captive.

A winner
is not afraid to contradict himself
when faced
with a contradictory situation;
a loser
is more concerned
with being consistent
than with being right.

A winner
appreciates the irony of fate,
and the fact
that merit is not always rewarded,
without becoming cynical;
a loser
is cynical
without appreciating
the irony of fate.

A winner
knows how to be serious
without being solemn;
a loser
is often solemn
as a substitute
for his lack of capacity
to be serious.

A winner
does what is necessary
with good grace,
saving his energy
for situations where he has a choice;
a loser
does what is necessary
under protest,
and has no energy left
for moral decisions.

A winner
recognizes that the only true authority
is moral authority;
a loser,
having little inner respect,
tries to assume more external authority
than his character can handle.

A winner
tries to judge his own acts
by their consequences,
and other people's acts
by their intentions;
a loser
gives himself all the best of it
by judging his own acts
by his intentions,
and the acts of others
by their consequences.

A winner
rebukes and forgives;
a loser
is too timid to rebuke
and too petty to forgive.

scoreboard
five

A winner
stops talking
when he has made his point;
a loser
goes on
until he has blunted his point.

A winner
makes every concession he can,
short of sacrificing his basic principles;
a loser
is so afraid
of making concessions
that he hangs on to pride
while his principles
go down the drain.

A winner
employs his defects
in the service of his assets;
a loser
subverts his assets
in the service of his defects.

A winner
acts the same
toward those who can be helpful,
and those who can be of no help;
a loser
fawns on the powerful
and snubs the weak.

A winner
wants the respect of others,
but does nothing with that end in mind;
a loser
does everything
with that end in mind,
and therefore defeats his purpose.

A winner
knows how much
he still has to learn,
even when he is considered an expert
by others;
a loser
wants to be considered an expert
by others
before he has even learned enough
to know how little he knows.

A winner's
saving grace
is the ability to laugh at himself
without demeaning himself;
a loser
privately deprecates himself
and therefore cannot publicly afford
to laugh at himself.

A winner
is sympathetic to weakness
in others,
because he understands
and accepts his own weakness;
a loser
is contemptuous
toward weakness in others,
because he despises
and rejects his own weaknesses.

A winner
hopes for a miracle
after everything else has failed;
a loser
hopes for a miracle
before anything has been tried.

A winner,
in the end,
gives more than he takes;
a loser
dies clinging to the illusion
that "winning" means taking
more than you give.

A winner
isn't afraid to leave the road
when he doesn't agree
with the direction it's taking;
a loser
follows "the middle of the road"
no matter where the road is going.